Worth
FAR MORE
THAN...

DIANNA OLSON *and*
CATHY HARTLEY

We dedicate this book to our mother. Although she never understood her true value, she was the very picture of God's grace and love. Thank you, Mom, for showing us how to walk in acceptance and kindness. Thank you for the times that you reminded us to stop and look at the wonder of God's creation. Thank you for teaching us about Jesus — the most valuable lesson of your life.

We Love You.

CONTENTS

PROVERBS 31: 10-31 (NIV)

A wife of noble character who can find? She is worth far more than rubies.

Her husband has full confidence in her and lacks nothing of value.

She brings him good, not harm, all the days of her life. She selects wool and flax and works with eager hands.

She is like the merchant ships, bringing her food from afar.

She gets up while it is still night; she provides food for her family and portions for her female servants.

She considers a field and buys it; out of her earnings she plants a vineyard.

She sets about her work vigorously; her arms are strong for her tasks.

She sees that her trading is profitable, and her lamp does not go out at night.

In her hand she holds the distaff and grasps the spindle with her fingers.

She opens her arms to the poor and extends her hands to the needy.

When it snows, she has no fear for her household; for all of them are clothed in scarlet.

She makes coverings for her bed; she is clothed in fine linen and purple.

Her husband is respected at the city gate, where he takes his seat among the elders of the land.

She makes linen garments and sells them and supplies the merchants with sashes.

She is clothed with strength and dignity; she can laugh at the days to come.

She speaks with wisdom, and faithful instruction is on her tongue.

She watches over the affairs of her household and does not eat the bread of idleness.

Her children arise and call her blessed; her husband also, and he praises her:

"Many women do noble things, but you surpass them all."

Charm is deceptive, and beauty is fleeting; but a woman who fears the Lord is to be praised.

Honor her for all that her hands have done, and let her works bring her praise at the city gate.

CHAPTER 1

Perspective

"We must reject not only the stereotypes
that others hold of us, but also the
stereotypes that we hold of ourselves."
— *Shirley Chisholm*

S o many women do not recognize, let alone appreciate, their true value. Life has a convincing way of teaching us that we are damaged goods — broken, unhappy and fear-filled — and that our challenging circumstances will never change. We would like to offer a new perspective.

DIANNA'S PERSPECTIVE

I'm a hot mess! Seriously, ONE HOT MESS! So, my sister, Cathy, was working with me through the book *Soul Care: 7 Transformational Principles for a Healthy Soul* by Rob Reimer. I highly recommend it. Fabulous book. Two enthusiastic thumbs-ups. During one of our meetings, I made a comment about really striving to make my husband, Gary, proud of me. I followed it with "You know, the Proverbs 31 woman and all that." To which Cathy responded, "Ugh!" (the sound she made was actually more of a guttural noise that I have no idea how to spell). That was not the response I was expecting.

We then discussed how that Bible passage has been used sometimes as a weapon against Christian women. She then asked me this simple question: "Do you actually want to be that woman?" What??? Of course, I want to be that woman! For crying out loud! I am a Christian woman. What else would I want to be other than the Proverbs 31 woman?

Then Cathy said the weirdest thing ever (surprising, because we have said some weird stuff to each other). She said, "I want to be Jael. You know, the woman that drove the tent stake into that guy's head." I don't know about you, but that does not sound like the Proverbs 31 woman. Nope, nothing about murder.

This gave me a lot to think about during the next few days. Such a simple question, but hugely profound, and so challenging to what I have always thought. Do I want to be that woman? I do not want to get up early, work all day, and then go to bed late. In fact, I have what I call "My Fall Schedule." To be honest, sometimes it's my year-round schedule. We live in the Midwest, so when the weather turns cold, I like to have my jammies on by about 5:00 p.m. (unless I have spent the entire day in them already) and tucked into bed with a good book by 8:00 p.m. Now, thinking about it, I could get up early and go to bed late if I took a nice four-hour nap starting at about 10:00 a.m. every day.

Also, there is no way that I would ever plant a vineyard. I do not have a green thumb. In fact, when Gary and I were first married 33 years ago, I was afraid to have children because I could not keep a plant alive. Now we have two fabulous kids who have grown into adults that we are very proud of. Turns out I would have done better with plants if they had just cried when they needed something. Do I want to be that woman?

A few nights later I was awake in the middle of the night. That question kept going through my mind. I got up and wrote the "Dianna 54 Woman," based on the "Proverbs 31 Woman." Why 54? you ask. Because I am 54 years old. (How did that happen so fast?) Some of you right now are running for a defibrillator. The audacity of this woman to rewrite Scripture! But stick with me. It was like something broke in me that night. Is it possible that God was trying to tell me that I am the Proverbs 31 Woman that He intended? I also realized I liked the Dianna 54 Woman. I'd be friends with her. This may not seem like a big deal to you, but one of the soul issues that Cathy and I were working on was that I spend a lot of time beating myself up for all of my flaws. Remember, I AM ONE HOT MESS! If the Dianna 54 Woman is me, and I like her, then maybe I am not as bad as I've told myself for so many years. MIND BLOWN!

I was so excited to share this with Cathy the following week. She loved it! This made me happy because I'm a people pleaser — just another one of my soul issues that we are working on. The only thing that would have been better is for her to have taken the paper and written a giant A+ in red ink at the top. We agreed that we didn't want this to end there. We wanted to hear other women's stories. Married, single, young, old, mothers, and women without children. We wanted to hear them all!

That was how this project was born. It's been amazing to see the reactions of the women we have asked to participate. Women who I thought had it all together. You know the ones. Every time you see them, they have huge smiles on their faces, their kids are well behaved in church, they don't call a pile of onion rings an onion salad with croutons and a side of ranch dressing just to feel better about their unwise choices, their clothes don't look like they slept in them (I'm lucky if I don't go to the grocery store with my shirt on backwards). But some of these put-together women were also struggling with the idea of the Proverbs 31 Woman.

One more thing that I want to explain. Why did we include "Cathy's Perspective" *and* "Dianna's Perspective"? The answer is simple. Cathy and I see things very differently. The best example I can think of is the time Cathy and her husband, John, were looking to buy a house in the small town that we grew up in after living in California for over 40 years. We asked what she was looking for, and she said a single-family dwelling. Um, do you mean a house? Same subject, different viewpoint. That is why two very different perspectives. Not because one is right, and the other is wrong. Simply different. That is what this project is all about. Celebrating our differences instead of trying to fit a mold.

CATHY'S PERSPECTIVE

Dianna *is* a hot mess! Seriously, ONE HOT MESS! Hah! Just kidding — kind of. If Dianna is a hot mess, then so am I, and so are you.

We are all somewhere on the path of figuring out God's plans and purposes for us and exactly who He, in His wisdom, designed us to be. Stop just a minute and take that in. You are divinely designed. YOU are divinely designed! In fact, look at Psalms 139:14: "I praise you, for I am fearfully and wonderfully made. Wonderful are your works; my soul knows it very well."

"Fearfully" here means "with great respect and honor" and "wonderfully made" means "distinct, unique, and set apart." You are divinely designed with great respect and honor and to be distinct and unique. That means that none of us can be copycat versions of someone else — not even the Proverbs 31 Woman. That is how this whole thing started. Sitting at the kitchen table that day with Dianna, I realized that my experience has been that she (Proverbs 31 lady) has been held up before us as the picture (the only picture?) of who we are supposed to be as God's girls. While we can respect her and even admire her, God made you to be you and only you.

Now, this idea can be either inspiring or daunting. After our conversation, Dianna took the initiative to write the "Dianna 54 Woman." The D54W is original, imaginative, and funny — just as Dianna is original, imaginative, and funny. It truly is the essence of who God created her to be. In this book, we have invited an eclectic collection of women to write their own version of the Proverbs 31 Woman. We call them Identity Declarations (IDs). As you read this book, listen carefully to the distinctly different voices speaking here. We hope that you will be inspired, at whatever age you are or whatever stage of life you are in, to courageously step out and fully embrace the woman that you are created to be.

By the way, I need to clarify something. Just in case you

are wondering, I do not choose to emulate Jael because she drove a tent stake through a guy's head, although there have been times . . .

No, I choose to be like Jael in that she stood strong in the face of intimidating circumstances, used resources at hand, and, well, drove a tent stake into a bad guy's head.

CHAPTER 2

God's Handiwork

"Learn to embrace your own unique beauty,
celebrate your unique gifts with confidence.
Your imperfections are actually a gift."
— *Kerry Washington*

This book offers you an opportunity to evaluate your life from a new viewpoint. We are sisters that see the world through very different lenses. Dianna is funny and whimsical, artistic, and defies categorization. Cathy is quite serious, studious, feels safest with structure, and loves big words. She once used the word "theodicy" in conversation. For those of you who are of normal intelligence:

The-od-icy, noun: the vindication of divine goodness and providence in view of the existence of evil.

Dianna had to look up the definition. Then she had to look up several words in the definition. So we were surprised that we were challenged to work together when the idea for this book dropped into our lap. We have gathered versions of the Proverbs 31 Woman from 21 women and have called them Identity Declarations (IDs). With this book, we hope that you find inspiration to write your own Identity Declaration — your own ID. When someone asks to see your ID, do you display it proudly? Has anyone ever taken a good driver's license photo? Do you hold it just right to make sure that your thumb is covering your weight, the number that is now your goal weight? Or is it just us? We want you to be proud and inspired by this ID, share it without reservation, even love your ID.

Some of you may be thinking, "I've got nothing." Nothing important to offer, no meaningful accomplishment, no substantial contribution to the world. It's difficult for you to even imagine being audacious enough to believe that you possess significant worth. We saw it often while writing this book. Women who, in our eyes, were women of consequence could not see, and therefore could not appreciate, their value.

While encouraging you to never, meaning *not ever*, permit anyone or anything to convince you to be anything other than the very best, authentic version of your astonishing self, let's speak to a few very real hindrances that can limit and prevent ID love.

Childhood can be, and often is, brutal. We have our want-them-to-be-perfect-never-are-perfect parents. News flash! Parents are people, and, as people, are prone to all human flaws and failings. If you are now a parent, you realize how ill-equipped we all are when we bring that first baby home. "Take her home," they say. "Keep her alive," they say. But you can't even figure out how to properly install the car seat for that ride home.

Not one person gets out of childhood unscathed. Well, maybe Jesus. But we aren't Him, are we? To those who have experienced flagrant and destructive emotional, physical, and sexual abuse while growing up, we want to express sincere empathy as you travel your life path. We believe that God can heal even the deepest of soul wounds, and we encourage you to reach out to someone who can help. To others, be aware that even seemingly trivial mistreatment can have a far-reaching impact and acutely injure our identity.

Children themselves, whether intentionally or unintentionally, are often unkind and insensitive. Being expressed as an inconsiderate word or by name-calling, jeering, or even physical aggression, these harms can set in place identity damage. As you read this, a name or situation may have come to your mind. It's amazing that no matter how much time has passed, most of us can still remember the hurtful things that have been said or done to us. Things that the person who caused the initial harm probably will never remember.

Let's face it, most elementary school-age children are not

the most eloquent or even intelligent beings. Why are we still affected by those words or deeds? Why have we allowed them to make an actual difference in our lives? These are hurts caused by people whose best retort was probably "No. Duh." It's probably time to let it go. In full disclosure, we are talking to ourselves right now as much as to you.

It's noteworthy, also, that there exists a very real enemy to the health of our soul. You think the mean kids in grade school are bad? This enemy wants to hinder and injure our way of being in the world. It wants to prevent us from living our best God-given, divinely designed life and devises weapons to accomplish just that. However, here is the truth: As powerful as the weapons of this enemy may seem, they have only the power that we allow. That enemy does not have the final say. God does, and this is what God says about you:

God has made us what we are (For we are his handiwork/ workmanship/work of art). In Christ Jesus, God made (created) us to do good works, which God planned in advance for us to live our lives doing. Ephesians 2:10 EXB

Take a breath. Right now, take a breath. We want to tell you that if you breathe in and breathe out, you have value. You have no idea, nor is it your business to know, how your words or actions might benefit someone else who may be struggling to take their breath today.

Yes, we just said that it is not your business to know how you impact other people. Let us explain what we mean. We have already established that God has created you "to do good works" according to His plan and purpose. That means that we have one job — to live a life that corresponds to those good works, which means that our life purpose is not to impact other people, but to live according to divine plan. If we live only to impact others, we will find it hard to find fulfillment and keep it, because how much impact is enough impact? How do we know if we are accomplishing our life work? When people are happy with us? When we are applauded, approved, and celebrated? What happens when we are no longer praised by those same people? Does that mean we are failing?

The Bible gives us a list of life standards: love, joy, peace, patience, kindness, goodness, faithfulness, gentleness, and self-control. Believe us when we tell you that as we live according to these standards, people will be positively impacted. Simply doing what we can to assist, comfort, support, or relieve can impact people and families for years to come, and they do not even need to know your name.

Mom told the story of their December 23, 1951, wedding night. After the wedding, which was attended by exactly four people — the bride, the groom, the pastor, and his wife — Dad, with his entire life savings of $400, and Mom in her bright-red winter coat, climbed into their Dodge and drove through the night to visit Dad's family in Arkansas. Dad thought they were going to be able to have a big time because he had his $400 in his pocket.

A few hours away from home, their car suddenly spun out of control in the ice and snow. Mom was thrown from the car, her bright-red coat vividly stark against the brilliant white of the snow. Thankfully, a caring couple stopped and helped the young newlyweds. Before continuing their own journey, these people made sure Mom and Dad were safe, even paying for their hotel room. A few days later, our parents made their way home, having used their entire $400 for car repair. Mom never knew the names of the people who stopped to help them, but she never forgot their loving-kindness.

We would like to encourage you today to look around. Is there someone you could help today? Just do what you can. Mother Teresa said, "I alone cannot change the world, but I can cast a stone across the waters to create many ripples."

The IDs we have included in this book are actual women in our lives. We greatly respect each one for their unique identities. They each were more transparent and vulnerable in this process than we ever expected, and we shed tears as we read. These are women whom we love, and we hope that while writing their IDs they came to love themselves more. Read them with a listening ear and you will discover that, although each used the same template, every voice is distinctly different.

Let us be very clear about one thing. It is not our intention to dishonor Scripture or any ministry. We believe wholeheartedly in Galatians 5:1: "It is for freedom's sake that Jesus set us free." That includes every person walking in the fullness of God's design. Seriously, if you know someone who can fully identify with the Proverbs 31 Woman, we want to meet them.

In the meantime, we have some questions. For instance, do you ever get angry (*really* angry) at those closest to you, even living in your household? Are you ever resentful? Do you ever find yourself wishing for more time, energy, or ambition to keep up with the demands of life? Do you ever despair of the possibility of fulfilling your divine purpose for living? Inquiring minds want to know!

We hope this book will help. It is intended to be experienced interactively, starting with the title. You will notice that it is intentionally not a full thought. You fill in the rest. What are you more valuable than? What holds worth in your life experience? Go ahead, figure it out. The goal is to help you realize how wonderfully fabulous you are. The template that we used is included in the back of this book. Use as much or as little as you wish. It's yours; make it personal. After you have read the contributions and completed the title, it will be time for you to express your own Identity Declaration.

One more thing before we dive into the IDs that we collected. This book is dedicated to our amazing mother. She truly never thought of herself as amazing. She grew up with very little money and even less confidence. But she made each of her children feel safe and loved. She is missed every day. We felt it only appropriate that we write an ID based on her. Read Charlene 83 Woman and get to know our remarkable mom.

CHAPTER 3

Identity Declarations

CHARLENE 83 WOMAN

A woman of noble character who can find?

She is worth more than unlimited Rice Krispie Treats.

Her husband had full confidence in her and lacked nothing of value, but he didn't realize that until much later in life.

She brought him good, not harm, all the days of her life.

She selected cake decorating supplies or painting supplies or doll-making supplies, depending on her hobby of the month, and worked with eager hands.

She was like a burgundy van, bringing her food from Walmart or McDonald's or Taco Bell, sometimes all in the same day.

She got up whenever she wanted, but when her kids were young, she got up early to wake everyone for school, usually with a song. She provided food for her family and portions for anyone who might need a little help,

She considered what was best for her family, sometimes to the detriment of her own needs.

She saw that her hobbies were profitable, and her house was never dark because the stove light was always on to welcome you home.

In her hands she held her Bible and was always ready to point out a verse with her bent arthritic fingers.

She opened her arms to the poor and extended her hands to the needy.

When it snowed, she had no fear for her household; for all of them were ready to dump everything at the door and put on warm clothes to go snowmobiling.

She bought whatever her household needed and some things that she wanted. She was clothed in every outfit that Farm & Fleet sold.

Her husband was respected in the city that they had made their home for more than 60 years, where he took his seat as a meticulous contractor.

She made wedding cakes, sold them and supplied kids' classrooms with cookies.

She was clothed with love and compassion; she could laugh at the days to come and many days in the past.

She spoke with profound wisdom, and faithful instruction was on her tongue.

She kept track of everything in her household and could pull out of a drawer anything you might have needed at any given moment.

Her children and thousands of Sunday school kids arose and called her blessed.

Her husband had this to say about her:

"I lost the love of my life on January 15, 2015," and he followed her six short weeks later.

Charm is deceptive, and beauty is fleeting; but a woman who fears the Lord is to be praised. She has received the reward she has earned and is now dancing with Jesus.

DIANNA 54 WOMAN

A wife of noble character who can find?

She is worth far more than a lifetime supply of cheese.

Her husband has full confidence in her and lacks nothing of value. She brings him good, not harm, all the days of her life.

She selects flour and sugar and works with eager hands.

She is like the 18-wheelers, bringing her food from Meijer or Walmart, depending on which has the best deals.

She gets up when she wakes up; she feeds her family and friends.

She considers rental property, and she and her husband buy it together. Out of the earnings she pays off the mortgage so that she and her husband will have income in their retirement.

She works hard to keep track of the day-to-day things in her household.

She opens her arms to the poor and extends her hands to the needy.

When it snows, she has no fear for her household; for they are clothed in fleece and heavy socks.

Her husband is respected by his peers, unless he tells a dad joke, but that's on him.

She is clothed with strength and dignity, but not always in a bra; she can laugh at the days to come.

She speaks with wisdom, and faithful instruction is on her tongue.

Her children, as long as they don't live with her, arise and call her blessed; her husband sometimes also notices.

Charm is deceptive, and beauty is fleeting; but a woman who fears the Lord is to be praised.

CATHY 68 WOMAN

A woman of noble character, who can find?

She is worth far more than the accolades of man.

Her circle of influence has full confidence in her and lacks nothing of value.

She brings them good, not harm, all the days of her life.

She selects thoughts and words and works with intentionality.

She scours books, bringing wisdom from many sources.

She gets up really, really early and loves to tell you that.

She considers the health of her soul, and out of her growth, she helps others mature.

Although her mind is not as quick as it used to be, she sets about her work with excitement.

She is diligent in her studies and has been called "wise."

Her husband is proud of her and unabashedly (and sometimes embarrassedly) brags about her.

She is clothed in jeans and a long-sleeved T-shirt; she can smile at the future because she trusts her God.

She manages the needs of her household, only irritably complaining when she is especially tired. She does not eat the bread of idleness, but she does eat her fair share of desserts.

Charm can deceive, and true beauty is a condition of the heart. The woman who reveres the One True God is to be admired. May she be given extravagant Love, Grace, and Mercy.

DEBBIE 53 WOMAN

A wife of noble character who can find?

She is worth far more than the morning's first cup of coffee or a rainy-day nap.

Her husband has full confidence in her and lacks nothing of value.

She brings him good, not harm, all the days of her life.

She selects spreadsheets and reports and works with eager hands.

She is like Door Dash, delivering food and necessities to her home (minus the tip).

She gets up after hitting the snooze button twice — but still gets to work on time.

She considers the greenest bananas for her husband and tastiest treats for her dog; out of her earnings she pays off her Kohl's card and saves the rest for later.

She opens her arms to the poor and extends her heart to the hurting.

When it snows, she has no fear for her household; for all are clothed in jeans, flannel shirts, and work boots.

Her husband is respected, and she is proud of the man he is.

She is clothed in strength and dignity; she can laugh at the days to come because God has put her broken pieces back together with a promise and a kiss on her head.

She speaks with wisdom, and encouragement is on her tongue.

Her child arises and calls her blessed — usually after she does his laundry:

"Many women do noble things, but you surpass them all."

Charm is deceptive, and beauty is fleeting; but a woman who fears the Lord is to be celebrated.

Recognize her for who she is, and let her compassion be your comfort at the city gate.

TAMI 42 WOMAN

Who can find a virtuous and capable woman?

She is more precious than chips and queso.

Her family can trust her, and she will greatly enrich their lives.

She brings them good, not harm, all the days of her life.

She finds deals at the thrift store and happily buys them.

She drives around town in her SUV, bringing food from multiple stores, depending on where the best deal is found.

She gets up early, occasionally before dawn, to prepare coffee so she can function and plan the day's work for her children.

She works two jobs and attends college. With her earnings she feeds and clothes a house full of children.

She is energetic and strong, a hard worker.

She makes sure her dealings are profitable; her lamp burns late into the night. But at times she falls asleep before her children do.

Her hands are busy serving those around her, her fingers scrubbing messes.

She extends a helping hand to the poor and opens her arms to the needy.

She has no fear of winter for her household; for everyone has warm clothes. Although, winter makes her grumpy because she loathes the cold.

She doesn't make her own bedspreads; she doesn't know how to sew.

She dresses in jeans and whatever shirt is clean in the closet.

She has been well known at the school district office, where she has fought for her kids to have what they needed.

She prepares food for her family and delights when they eat the leftovers.

She is clothed with strength and dignity; and she laughs without fear of the future.

When she speaks, she hopes her words are wise, and she gives instructions with kindness until she has to repeat herself numerous times because her children "didn't hear" her.

She carefully watches over everything in her household but suffers at times from procrastination.

Her children, before age eleven and after age fourteen, stand and bless her.

Charm is deceptive, and beauty does not last; but a woman who fears the Lord is to be praised.

"I am learning every day to allow
the space between where I am
and where I want to be to inspire
me and not terrify me."
— *Tracee Ellis Ross*

AMBER 43 WOMAN

A woman of noble character who can find?

She is worth far more than rose gold.

Her husband has full confidence in her and lacks nothing, period. She is honest with him always and never has bad intentions for him all the days of his life.

She selects pretty flowers and uses twine to work eagerly with her hands.

She is like a weightlifter bringing in all the grocery bags on one arm, in one trip, from the car.

She gets up before her alarm goes off at five every day whether she wants to or not.

She faithfully puts her quarter in at Aldi's (to rent her grocery cart) every Saturday morning, bringing food to her family and her fur babies.

She instructs little souls, which she loves to do, and gets paid for it; because of her earnings, her children get to do all the extras.

She sees that her studies are profitable, and her phone stays charged at night.

In her hand she holds her notebook and one of the good pens in her fingers.

When it snows, she has no fear for her household, because she has given up trying to make them wear their coats.

Her husband is respected at work, where he hustles daily for his family.

She is clothed in robes of righteousness, which gives her strength to walk into the future, and she is not intimidated by it.

Her words are kind, and she's got jokes.

Her children wake up and give her kisses. Her husband does, too, as long as she doesn't come in too bubbly in the morning:

"Many women do noble things, but you surpass them all."

Charm is deceptive and beauty is fleeting; but mascara and waxing are doing the trick for now!

BETHANY 41 WOMAN

A gal of tenacious character who can find?

She is worth more than comparing herself to others.

She is growing in confidence and learning that she has all she needs.

She brings smiles, not harm, all the days of her life (except when she doesn't, and then she apologizes as quickly as possible).

She makes the best choices she can and offers grace to herself when she doesn't.

She gets up when her eyes open and spends intentional time with her daughter and cares for herself and her community.

She considers growth areas for her soul. Out of her earnings she has time to support other sojourners.

She sees that her soul work is producing permanent growth, and her ability to be vulnerable is growing.

She holds the checkbook and manages the budget with wisdom and tact.

She opens her table to friends and family and gives to those in need.

No matter the weather, she has no fear for her household.

The dynamic duo of her hustle and God's faithfulness never leaves a void.

She makes morning breakfast and ensures the house is tidy for her Nana to enjoy.

Her husband is physically, emotionally, and mentally strong, bringing a smile to her face with his intentionality and passionate love. He is respected in the kitchen and provides wisdom in his men's' group. He learns mightily from his community.

She runs her business and tasks with focus and determination.

She is clothed in jeans and a soft T-shirt; she can laugh at the days to come in comfort.

She speaks with levity, and humor is on her tongue.

She watches over her responsibilities, takes risks, and walks in courage.

Her daughter loves to snuggle her; her husband loves her challenging personality:

"Many women do noble things, but you surpass them all."

Charm is deceptive, and beauty is fleeting, but a woman who fears the Lord is to be praised.

Give her the reward she has earned, and let her find her identity in Christ and be filled with the true love of the Father.

TARA 30 WOMAN

A woman of noble character who can find?

She is worth far more than the new, cool Vans she wants to buy.

Her dog, Tito, has full confidence in her and lacks nothing of value.

She brings him good, not harm, all the days of her life (unless he catches another possum; then he's on his own).

She selects wood and sandpaper and turns the lathe with eager hands.

She is like merchant ships, bringing her handmade artistry to markets.

She gets up when it is still dark (only because she has bills to pay). She provides a smile to strangers and support to her friends.

She designs exhibits; out of her earnings she buys Taco Bell.

She sets about her work vigorously; her arms are strong for her tasks.

She sees no limit to what she can create, and her lamp she made by hand.

In her hand she holds her Rollerblades and grasps her backpack full of snacks and activities with her fingers.

She opens her arms to all children and extends her hands to those who feel like they don't fit.

When it snows, she has no fear for her household, for all of them are clothed in layers because the dog still needs a walk!

She puts her hair in space buns; she is adorned with her handmade earrings.

Her friends are proud of her growth and push her to keep moving forward.

She makes just about anything and surprises those close to her with thoughtful gifts.

She is outfitted with stubbornness and bravery; she can laugh at the days to come.

She speaks with encouragement, but listening is more her jam.

She watches over her houseplants and waters them when they're thirsty.

Her friends text her and call her blessed:

"Many women do noble things, but you surpass them all."

Charm is deceptive, and beauty is fleeting, but a woman who fears the Lord is to be praised.

Give her the reward she has earned, and let her work bring her freedom to express who God created her to be.

PEGGY 61 WOMAN

A woman of character who can find?

She is worth more than a walk in the woods.

Her Jesus is full of confidence in her and lacks nothing of value. She brings Him praise and thanks all the days of her life.

She selects chia and flax and blends them in her morning smoothie.

She shops at the local grocery, carefully reading labels.

She gets up while it is still morning; she provides tasty delights for her family and treats for her friends.

She considers a trail and walks it; out for adventure she plants each foot.

In her hands she holds hiking poles and lightly grasps the handles with her fingers.

She sets about her trek vigorously; her legs are exhausted from her task. She sees her journey is accomplished and is eager for her lamp to go out at night.

She opens her arms to the poor and extends her hands to the needy.

When it snows, she has no fear — she loads the car and heads south. She shields her eyes with sunglasses; she is clothed in a hoodie and shorts.

Her Jesus is worshipped at her gatherings, where He takes His place in the hearts of His people.

She is retired and lives by a loose schedule.

She is clothed in strength and a smile; she can laugh at days gone by.

She seeks wisdom, and faithful instructions she is eager to hear.

She watches over the affairs of her household and enjoys being active.

Her friends arise and call her blessed; her Jesus also, and He loves her.

Many women do noble things; she hopes to learn from them all.

Charm is deceptive, beauty is fleeting, but a woman who fears the LORD is to be cherished. Honor the LORD for all His hand has done; let His works bring Him praise at the city gate.

"A really strong woman accepts
the war she went through and
is ennobled by her scars."
— *Carly Simon*

JEANNETTE 62 WOMAN

An excellent wife who can find?

Only Jesus can!

He is removing the ashes and rubble of her broken life, gloriously revealing her beauty more precious than rubies.

Her husband is being invited to trust her as God transforms her life.

Surrendering the tyranny of her "measure up now" list, she works in the presence of Jesus, singing for joy.

She is frugal and health conscious, bringing her food from surprising sources.

She rises in the dark quiet of early morning to enjoy being with Jesus, receiving abundant treasures to share with others.

She extends her hands to the poor and opens her heart to the lost and lonely.

She is overcoming fears of chilling trials in her family knowing that God listens to her prayers and offers His radiant love to them.

She enjoys the hunt for beautiful clothing in resale shops, garments designed and put there just for her.

Her husband is known for his keen mind, clever humor, and generous heart.

She joyously shares the produce of her farm to spread God's goodness.

When she meditates on the mercy of God toward all, and that He has clothed her with Christ, she smiles at the future.

With every graying hair, she is learning more the beauty and power of speaking words of life with wisdom and kindness.

Eating the bread of idle despair is a weakness, and she is forever grateful that God is perfecting His overcoming power in her.

God is tuning her heart to hear His praise overflowing through many sources, cheering her on in the race she runs.

And, as she enters His gates with thanksgiving, all the gifts of His ordained works are singing for joy.

Listen! He is beautiful! He is coming!

KATY 34 WOMAN

A wife of noble character who can find?

She is worth far more than the number on the scale.

Her family has full confidence in her and lacks nothing of value.

She brings them good, not harm, all the days of her life.

She selects peanut butter and jelly and works with eager hands.

She is like a minivan bringing her packed lunches to the masses.

She gets up every time her bladder tells her to and often doesn't return to sleep.

She considers the hours of her day and plans them carefully. Out of her work she reaps homework and extra snuggles.

She opens her arms to the lonely and extends her hands to the small.

When it snows, she has no fear for her household; for they are clothed in an extra layer of hand-me-downs.

She makes extra runs to the grocery store; she is often clothed in yesterday's athleisure wear.

She speaks in Disney movie quotes, and gentle correction is on her tongue.

Her children rise up and call her blessed — unless she says no to a 16th Band-Aid. Her husband protects and cares for her as they work together.

Charm is deceptive, and beauty is fleeting; but a woman who fears the Lord is to be praised. Give her the reward she's earned, and let her work bring her favor in the eyes of Jesus.

CAROL 80 WOMAN

A nurse, bookkeeper, housekeeper, cook, gardener, travel planner, and all-around wife of noble character who can find?

She is worth far more than the money in the U.S. Mint.

Her husband believes she can hang the moon and wonders when she will get that award of value.

She selects her Cricut, tons of paper, vinyl, and ink and works with eager hands.

She is like a miracle worker, bringing her food from the bulk stores and making it all come together into something palatable.

When she gets up, which is usually in the morning, she provides food for her hungry husband and portions for all the birds, squirrels, and whatever other wild animal shows up.

She considers her family's needs and buys them out of the earnings from her crafts. She plants seeds of kindness in others' lives the same way.

She questions whether her trading is profitable, so she keeps working late into the night.

She holds the laptop from which she creates her designs and grasps the Cricut tools with her hands.

She opens her hands to those who have baggage that needs sorting and uses her training to help them overcome their pain.

When it snows, she lets everyone concerned know she will be doing only crafts that day and staying toasty warm.

She makes handmade quilts for others' beds and is clothed by Goodwill, Salvation Army, and other resale shops.

She speaks from experience, and healing is on her tongue.

She watches every penny in her house and makes her own bread.

Her children are her encouragement, and she knows she is blessed. Her husband is sadly missed but left much of his sense of humor around.

Many women do normal things, but most women go far beyond.

Charm doesn't work on me, and beauty depends on the time of the day, but I greatly fear and love the Lord, and He is to be praised. If I have earned a reward, let me appreciate that it was only by the Grace of God.

TRISH 26 WOMAN

An agent of noble character who can find?

She is worth far more than historical documents.

Her co-workers have full confidence in her and lack nothing of value.

She brings them good, not harm, all the days of her life.

She selects guns and badges and works with eager hands.

She is like a motorcade, protecting persons of high rank.

She gets up based on others' schedules. She provides joy to a lonely place and peace for those with no faith.

She trains diligently among men; out of her earnings she buys a place to call her home.

She sets about her work vigorously; her arms are strong for her tasks.

She sees that her hard work is sought after, and her phone never stops ringing.

In her hand she holds the rifle and pulls the trigger with her finger, perfectly hitting the target.

She opens her arms to the mentally ill and extends her hands to families confused about where their loved ones have wandered to.

When it snows, she has no fear for her household, for all of them are clothed in gray sweatpants and gray sweatshirts, the typical groutfit.

She makes refurbished pieces out of old treasures; she is clothed in material from the 1960s, now referred to as "boho-chic."

Her parents are respected in the home where she grew up. When she visits, it stirs in her a longing to return.

She lifts dumbbells and kettlebells and supplies the other agents with competition.

She is clothed in strength and dignity; she can laugh at the days to come.

She speaks with humility, and accountability is on her tongue.

She watches over the rumors of her workplace and does not fall into the mischief of poor tactics.

Her parents arise and call her blessed; her sisters also, and they pray for her:

"Many women do noble things, but you surpass them all."

Charm is deceptive, and beauty is fleeting; but a woman who fears the Lord is to be praised.

MACKENZIE 30 WOMAN

A woman of noble character who can find?

She is worth far more than stacks and stacks of books.

Her husband has full confidence in her and lacks nothing of value.

She brings him good, not harm, all the days of her life.

She selects puzzles and video games and works with eager hands.

She is like a ferry, allowing herself to take her time to enjoy the journey and getting to wherever she needs to whenever she arrives.

She gets up whenever her son wakes up but stays up as late as she can to get the alone time she requires.

She provides an all-you-can-eat buffet for her breastfed son and food from Aldi and Costco for everyone else.

She is a stay-at-home momma.

She loves and cares for her expanding zoo: son, dog, cat, and fish.

She sets about her work vigorously; her arms are strong for her tasks.

In her hands she holds her son and her latest book from her reading list. She sees that she is a homebody and introvert, but once the ice is broken, she is a loyal friend (who may take some time texting you back).

She opens her arms with love and compassion to all those around her by sharing her life and home.

When it snows, she has no fear for her household; for they reside in the warm Florida sun.

She is clothed in leggings and a T-shirt.

Her husband is respected where he counsels and educates to promote healing.

She makes delicious tea while paying the bills and supplies the home with organization and clean laundry.

She is called wise and is slow to make decisions, but once made, she is all in. She is a prayer warrior who quietly fights for all those in her life. She smiles at the future, for she knows Jesus has her in His hands.

She watches over the affairs of her household and works diligently to grow and become a healthier version of herself.

Her children arise and call her blessed; her husband also, and he praises her.

Charm is deceptive, and beauty is fleeting, but a woman who fears the Lord is to be praised.

"Women are like tea bags.
We don't know our true strength
until we are in hot water."
— *Eleanor Roosevelt*

CHRISTY 64 WOMAN

A business owner, wife, and mother of noble character who can find?

She is worth far more than Bitcoin.

Her employees, customers, and family have full confidence in her, and they lack nothing of value.

She brings them good, not harm, all the days of her life.

She selects investments, insurance plans, and advertising while on the computer. She works with eager hands.

She is like a fleet of Amazon vans gathering and distributing her latest purchases from Menards (collecting rebates) and items from Kohl's (using her Kohl's Cash).

She gets up when it is dark as the coffee machine sounds the alarm and she smells the aroma of coffee. She provides prayers for her business, employees, and family, to whom she adds a text of encouragement for the day.

She listens to Cramer (CNBC) for stock tips and adds to her portfolio and the employees' 401(k). CNBC and Fox News keep her informed on world events.

She sets about her work vigorously; her arms are strong for her tasks.

She sees that her stock account is doing well, and her business is profitable. She checks in at night with each of her children to know how to pray for them and sends a kiss face emoji.

In her hand she holds a mouse for the computer, and in the kitchen a veggie slicer and Instant Pot are ready to prepare a counter of food.

She opens her arms to the poor and extends her hands to the needy.

When it snows, she has no fear for her household, for all of them are clothed in Carhartt from Blain's Farm & Fleet.

She makes financial decisions; she is clothed in anything she can buy on sale.

Her family and business are respected in the community; her husband is known and liked by all.

She gathers items for fund raisers and volunteers her time in her church and community.

She is clothed in strength and dignity; she can laugh at the days to come.

She speaks with wisdom (and a little sarcasm), and faithful instruction or recommendations are on her tongue.

She watches over the details of her business and her family and does not eat the bread of idleness (or any bread because of the gluten).

Her children arise and call her blessed at times; her husband is grateful for her but doesn't let her know:

"Many women do noble things, but you surpass them all."

Charm is deceptive, and beauty is fleeting, but a woman who fears the Lord is to be praised.

KELSEY 30 WOMAN

A hot-mess-express momma of noble character who can find?

She is worth far more than all the Starbucks coffee a mom needs to survive.

Her husband, three young kids, and pup have full confidence in her and lack nothing of value.

She brings them good, not harm, all the days of her life.

She selects her cleaning rags and overly used vacuum and works with eager hands.

She is like her crumb-filled Tahoe, bringing her food from Aldi for a deal.

She gets up when the first kid cries for food or needs a diaper change. She provides fruit snacks for when the kids whine, and wine and chocolate for nights with other mom friends.

She considers writing children and adult books and becoming an author one day; out of her earnings she would build a farmhouse with a large wraparound porch.

She sets about her work vigorously; her arms are strong for her tasks.

She sees that her house is put back in order each night from the tornado of toys everywhere, and her coffee machine is filled with water and ready for the morning.

In her hands she holds the "toy jail" clear container to help set rules and guidelines for sharing between her two toddlers.

She opens her arms to the other hot-mess mommas struggling to persevere and extends her hand to other families who need extra prayer for parenting young children.

When it snows, she has no fear for her household, for all of them are clothed in the mismatched clothes they chose (husband included) because that wasn't a battle she had in her to fight that day.

She makes blanket forts for her bed; she is clothed in oversized sweatshirts and her black leggings on repeat.

Her family is respected in her kid-filled neighborhood, where everyone shares old toys and opens their garages and backyards for afternoon playtime.

She makes "at-home school time" and supplies the kids with fun activities to make the days exciting and keep her sane and to pass the hours on some long days.

She is clothed in the same raggedy, hole-filled sweatshirt that has bleach on it and sweatpants that have a tiny hole in the knee. She can laugh at the realness of being a mom, with the honesty of it all, and at the days to come.

She speaks with honesty to other moms so they feel they can open up as well, so truthfulness is always on her tongue.

She watches over the mounds of constant laundry to make it disappear and does not compare her life to other moms, knowing Jesus put us all in different situations to "mom" through.

Her three sticky-fingered, sometimes stinky, but absolutely adorable kids arise and call her blessed; her hardworking husband, extremely loving dad to her kids, and wonderful leader of her family also praises her:

"Many women do noble things, but you surpass them all."

Charm is deceptive, and beauty is fleeting, but a woman who fears the Lord is to be praised.

Give her the reward she has earned, and let her work bring her a household full of crazy chaos, lots of giggles, smiles, and love overflowing within her family, which loves Jesus and all He blesses her with daily.

ANNETTE 62 WOMAN

A woman of noble character who can find?

She is worth far more than her weight in Häagen-Dazs.

Her family has full confidence in her and lacks nothing of value.

She brings them good, not harm, all the days of her life.

She selects yeast- and gluten-free flour and hopes it works out.

She is like DoorDash, bringing her food to anyone who will eat it.

She gets up when her dogs, Sophie and Sawyer, require her to; she provides food for her family and excessive treats for her dogs.

She is still a teacher at heart and takes any opportunity to make things into a fun lesson.

She sets about her work vigorously and always has more to do than time allows.

She sees that the freezer is full and very seldom runs out of chocolate chip cookies.

In her hand she holds a hoe and plants her garden with care (so she can make salsa later).

She opens her arms to everyone and says, "Welcome to our chaos!"

When it snows, her family will build a great snowman because they are just fun like that.

She is clothed in yoga pants and a hand me down sweatshirt.

Her husband is respected at the local track, where he takes his seat among the coaches of the city and is revered by countless tracksters.

She speaks with wisdom, and encouraging words are on her tongue.

She grocery shops, cleans, does laundry, schedules events, makes waffles for her grandchildren, and seldom sits down. (She doesn't seem to have the time or inclination to "just do nothing.")

Her children arise and call her clumsy; her husband, also, but later assures her that she just tries to move too fast.

Charm is deceptive, and beauty may have already flown, but a woman who fears the Lord is to be praised.

DEANNA 59 WOMAN

A woman of noble character who can find?

She is worth more than a tropical vacation.

Her family and friends have full confidence in her and never have to wonder where she stands.

She brings them honesty and encouragement all the days of her life.

She selects paints, carpet, and furniture and works with tight budgets all the time.

She is like an Amazon delivery truck, bringing bargains from afar.

She gets up when it is still dark but provides takeout food for her family because she doesn't cook.

She works with builders and architects and out of her earnings provides the "extras" for her family.

She rarely sits still and loves nothing better than a good plan. She makes draperies and pillows. She is clothed in jeans and a cute top.

She sees that her creativity is valued and works to bring enjoyment and comfort to others. She volunteers at church and strives to be generous and kind to her stepmother.

When it snows, she has no fear for her household because she knows how to run the snowblower.

Her husband is respected by all and adored by his daughters; deemed very funny by those who know him best.

She walks in faith and hope and believes the best days are yet to come.

She seeks wisdom and works to guard her tongue.

She organizes her household and tries to do something productive while watching TV.

Her daughters arise and call her Deanna because they want to get her attention.

Charm is deceptive, and beauty is fleeting; but a woman who fears the Lord is to be praised.

"If you're one of those people who has that little voice in the back of her mind saying, 'Maybe I could do [fill in the blank],' don't tell it to be quiet. Give it a little room to grow, and try to find an environment it can grow in."
— *Reese Witherspoon*

SARAH 34 WOMAN

The Woman Who Fears the Lord

An excellent wife who can find?

She is far more precious than the latest technology or NFTs.

The heart of her husband trusts in her, and together they are a power couple.

She speaks well of him and is continuously impressed with him all the days of her life.

She finds beautiful things and creates a peaceful home.

She is like the ships of the merchant; she stimulates the economy by buying brand-new things and then donating rejected items to thrift stores.

She rises while it is yet night and simultaneously provides income for her household and healthcare to patients.

She considers a project; with the fruit of her (and sometimes mostly husband's) hands, she completes them.

She dresses herself with strength and makes her arms strong by repositioning patients in their beds (and her shoulders are looking pretty darn good). She perceives that her intelligence and compassion can be helpful. She cares for vulnerable and sick people for long hours.

She puts her hands to the computer, and her hands hold the stethoscope. She opens her hands to the sick and reaches out her hands to the depressed.

She is not afraid of snow, for all her household are clothed in base layers and love winter.

She knits bed coverings for herself and those she loves; her clothing is chic and comfortable, with pockets.

Her husband is known as a great leader when he sits among the doctors and nurses of the healthcare field.

She coaches patients to live well; she tries to stay up-to-date on the latest research.

Strength and dignity are her clothing, and determination has gotten her further than she could imagine.

She opens her mouth with hypotheses backed by evidence, and the teaching of compassion is on her tongue.

She looks well to the ways of her household and orders groceries to be delivered.

Her child rises up and calls her "Mommy"; her husband calls her smart and sexy, and he praises her:

"Your compassion is deep and beautiful, and you keep me grounded."

Charm can be deceitful, and beauty can be vain, but a woman who fears the Lord is to be praised (and it's definitely still okay if she enjoys being charming and beautiful). Give her the doctorate she worked hard for, and let the kind words of her family, friends, and patients be cherished.

LAURA 65 WOMAN

A good woman is hard to find.

Her husband trusts her but can sometimes be a little nervous about it.

She's never spiteful and treats her man generously always.

She shops around for the best quality and prices for household things.

She doesn't need to get up before her family as she prepared the night before. When she does get up, she's ready to get going on the day's work.

She's skilled in the art of homemaking.

She's quick to assist anyone in need.

She doesn't worry about her family as the seasons change as their wardrobes and house are set.

Her husband is greatly respected in the many fields of knowledge and skill he has acquired.

She is clothed with strength and dignity.

Her children call her (or text her) often. Her husband calls all the time:

"Many women do wonderful things — and she sometimes is one of them!"

Charm is deceitful, and beauty is fleeting, but a little makeup helps slow that down.

But the woman who fears the Lord is to be praised!

SUSAN 61 WOMAN

A divorced-x-2 woman of noble character who can find?

She is worth far more than she knows or understands.

Her daughters, six grandchildren, and her rat terrier sometimes have full confidence in her and lack nothing of value.

She brings them good, not harm, all the days of her life.

She selects great puzzles and fun presents for her family and works with eager hands.

She is like her red Mazda CX5, bringing her food from Safeway, Walmart, or Sprouts.

She gets up well after sunrise because she prefers sunsets; she provides food for herself, family, and friends, and portions for her little beggar-dog, Rubie.

She considers getting a job but decides to volunteer instead; out of her earnings she plants a small, raised garden bed in Arizona and gives to help others.

She sets about her work at home and elsewhere vigorously; her arms are strong for her tasks.

She sees that her financial advisors are profitable, and her battery-operated candles do not go out at night.

In her hand she holds the weight of her family with her fingers and in her heart.

She opens her arms to the poor and extends her hands to the needy.

When it snows, she has no fear for her household, for all of them are clothed in the generous things God has provided for them.

She makes the coverings for her bed clean because she can't sew a lick; she is clothed in comfy clothes but will dress up if she must.

Her children are respected where they live and work, and she is very proud of them.

She makes people with diabetes glad they have diabetes and supplies the knowledge to live well with their diagnosis.

She is clothed in strength, which is sometimes called stubbornness, and at times dignity; she can laugh (almost always) at the days to come.

She speaks (God helping) with wisdom, and faithful instruction is sometimes on her tongue.

She watches over the affairs of her single household and does not eat the bread of idleness but does eat bread.

Her children, she hopes, arise and call her blessed, and the rest of her family, also, and they praise her:

"Many women do noble things, but you surpass them all."

Charm is deceptive, and beauty is fleeting, but a woman who fears the Lord is to be praised.

Give her the reward she has earned, and let her work bring her praise wherever she lives and serves.

STEPHANIE 56 WOMAN

A matriarch of noble character who can find?

She is worth far more than rubies.

Her husband is her biggest fan and does not mind embellishing the truth sometimes when talking about her.

She brings him good, not harm, sometimes at the expense of her own good.

She chooses joy and encouragement for a purpose.

She is like a cargo plane ready to deliver as needed.

She gets up when she feels rested so she can be at her best if her family and friends need her.

She oversees her household and business finances so she and her husband can give back to help others.

She sets her mind to entrepreneurial ideas and invokes that passion in others, at times providing her skills and labor to get them started.

She sees that her joy is contagious and will sometimes pretend so that others will catch it.

She opens her arms to the poor and extends her hands to the needy.

When it snows, she has no fear for anyone of her family, for she is known for hanging on to things, so there are always plenty of coats to go around.

Her husband is respected by her family for how hard he works to provide beyond what is necessary.

She makes music. She makes old furniture new again.

She is clothed in black stretch pants and sometimes the same pair for days; she can laugh when the thighs wear out.

She speaks with compassion unless she is crabby and must repent.

She watches over the affairs of her household and everyone else's to a fault.

Her children arise and call her often; her husband, also, mostly because they need something. They do call her blessed and they do praise her:

"Many women do noble things, but you surpass them all."

Charm is deceptive, and beauty is fleeting; but a woman who fears the Lord is to be praised.

CHAPTER 4

Tag! You're It!

"I'd rather regret the risks that didn't work
out than the chances I didn't take at all."
— *Simone Biles*

Now it's your turn! Write your own ID. A copy of
the template that we used with our participants
is included in this book. Also included are some
blank writing pages. Yes, it's okay to write in this book.
Remember, it is meant to be interactive. We promise that a
librarian is not going to show up at your house to issue you
a fine. (But, if a librarian does show up, we had nothing to
do with it, and we recommend you call the police.)

We hope you will take the time to use the template and rework it so that it speaks to your reality. Who are you, right now, as you are? We are not interested in an idealized version of yourself. We want to know you. We believe that we are all so fabulously different, and that is beautiful. We believe and hope that this gives us permission to fully embrace exactly who God designed us to be. We are all a work in progress. Cut yourself some slack. The Hemphills wrote the song "He's Still Working on Me." The chorus says:

"He's still working on me
To make me what I need to be
It took Him just a week to make the moon and the stars
The sun and the earth and Jupiter and Mars
How loving and patient He must be
'Cause He's still workin' on me."

Can we agree to enjoy (or at least, try to enjoy) the process of God making us exactly into what He had in mind when He created each of us?

Because there is not a controlling bone in our bodies (this statement is completely tongue-in-cheek; we can both be quite bossy if we aren't careful), you do not have to use the template, just loosely follow the Proverbs 31 idea.

Some of you may really struggle with this project. As good Christian women, we have sometimes confused honesty with pride. Is the statement "Don't get above your raising" familiar to you? When someone compliments you, do you automatically shut it down? Do you answer with reasons why that compliment is not true? Or, again, is that just us? There is a difference between being arrogant and rejoicing in the way that God has made us each so differently wonderful. Some of you may struggle to find good things to write about yourself. If you are one of those people, we would like for you to ignore the voices in your head. Ask God to bring to light His view of you. You may want to grab a trusted friend and work through it together. Or even write one for each other.

Write your ID, have fun, be creative, and let your voice be heard!

Here is the template and some ideas to get you started. We have underlined a few words and phrases that you may want to personalize. Have fun and make it your own!

- Wife — Woman or any other descriptive word you want to use
- Rubies — Something you value highly
- Husband — Kids, friends, boss
- Wool and flax — Two items that you work with often
- Merchant ships — Form of transportation
- When it is still dark — When do you get up?
- Portions for her servant girls — People who rely on you
- Considers a field and buys it — What is your vocation? (Don't you dare say just a housewife or just a

stay-at-home mom. It would cost over $110,000 to hire people to do all you do! We looked it up!)

- She plants a vineyard — What do you do with your vocation?

Okay, you get the idea.
Bless You, Amazing Woman!

First Name_____ Age_____ Woman

A <u>wife</u> of noble character who can find?

She is worth far more than <u>rubies</u>.

Her <u>husband</u> has full confidence in her and lacks nothing of value.

She brings him good, not harm, all the days of her life.

She selects <u>wool and flax</u> and works with eager hands.

She is like <u>merchant ships</u>, bringing her <u>food from afar</u>.

She gets up <u>when it is still dark</u>; she provides <u>food for her family</u> and <u>portions for</u> <u>her servant girls</u>.

She <u>considers a field and buys it</u>; out of her earnings <u>she plants a vineyard</u>.

She sets about her work vigorously; her arms are strong for her tasks.

She sees that her <u>trading is profitable</u>, and her <u>lamp does not go out at night</u>.

In her hand she holds the distaff and grasps the spindle with her fingers.

She opens her arms to the poor and extends her hands to the needy.

When it snows, she has no fear for her household; for all of them are clothed in scarlet.

She makes coverings for her bed; she is clothed in fine linen and purple.

Her husband is respected at the city gate, where he takes his seat among the elders of the land.

She makes linen garments and sells them, and supplies the merchants with sashes.

She is clothed in strength and dignity; she can laugh at the days to come.

She speaks with wisdom, and faithful instruction is on her tongue.

She watches over the affairs of her household and does not eat the bread of idleness.

He children arise and call her blessed; her husband also, and he praises her:

"Many women do noble things, but you surpass them all."

Charm is deceptive, and beauty is fleeting; but a woman who fears the Lord is to be praised. Give her the reward she has earned, and let her works bring her praise at the city gate.

After you have written your ID, you are invited to our Facebook page, "Worth Far More Than" to introduce yourself and share your experience. We want to meet you! Feel free to share your ID, insights you gained or struggles you encountered.

DISCUSSION QUESTIONS

➢ What did you learn about yourself while writing your ID?

➢ What surprised you while writing your ID?

➢ What section did you struggle with? Why?

➢ What section was easier than you thought it would be? Why?

➢ What do you like about your ID?

➢ What, if anything, bothers you about your ID?

➢ Who would you recommend this book to?

CHAPTER 5

Book Bloopers

At the beginning of this book, we told you that we, Cathy and Dianna, are very different people. So different that we were shocked that God put us together for this project! We thought we would back up this statement with some examples of what we are calling "Book Bloopers."

Dianna wanted to use Bible verses to divide the sections instead of the inspirational quotes from women. What could be better than Bible verses? Here are some examples of the ones she recommended:

Ezekiel 4:12. "Eat the food as you would a loaf of barley bread; bake it in the sight of the people, using human excrement for fuel."

Galatians 5:12. "Would that those who are upsetting you might also castrate themselves!"

2 Kings 2:23-24. "From there Elisha went up to Bethel.

As he was walking along the road, some boys came out of the town and jeered at him. 'Get out of here, baldy!' they said. 'Get out of here, baldy!' He turned around, looked at them, and called down a curse on them in the name of the Lord. Then two bears came out of the woods and mauled forty-two of the boys."

Deuteronomy 25:11-12. "If two men are fighting and the wife of one of them comes to rescue her husband from his assailant, and she reaches out and seizes him by his private parts, you shall cut off her hand. Show her no pity."

➢ Cathy said, "No."

Dianna wanted to actually name the kids who said mean things about her in grade school. Oh, and maybe a couple of guys who dumped her in high school.

➢ Cathy said, "No."

Dianna wanted to have Glamour Shots made for bio pictures. Complete with big hair, bare shoulders, and netting surrounding an overly made-up face.

➢ Cathy said, "No."

Dianna wanted to include the line "Slap the snot out of your husband" into the text of this book.

➢ Cathy said, "No."

Dianna wanted to include this discussion question: Who would win at mud wrestling, Cathy or Dianna? (The correct answer is Dianna)

➤ Cathy said, "No."

Moral of this story: Cathy is a killer of fun!

P.S. Dianna wrote this section.
Cathy said, "No!"

Made in the USA
Monee, IL
13 October 2022